A female northern cardinal cleans her red wings with a quick splash in the river.

KT-164-721

Northern Cardinal

Water helps wash away the dirt on this cardinal's wings. She will then preen her feathers with her beak until they are smooth and glossy again. Female cardinals only have red on their crests, wings and tails, but males have red on their bodies and heads too.

Polar Bear

Polar bears are built to swim, so it's no surprise they love to plunge into the ice-cold Arctic Ocean.

As this polar bear uses his paddle-like paws to swim, he turns the water into frothy white bubbles.

SPLASH

Camilla de la Bédoyère

QED

It's time to cool off! Mummy elephant uses her trunk to suck up water from the shallow river and splashes it over her baby.

Asian Elephant

Elephants live in hot places, so a cooling dip is always welcome. Asian elephants live in families and visit the local river every day to bathe.

Penguins flap their flippers in the frothy ocean waves.

Emperor Penguin

Penguins are water-loving birds that speed
through the ocean using flipper-like wings.
They stay on land to rest, meet their mates,
lay eggs and look after their chicks.

Dolphins have flippers and fins to
help them swim. They look like
fish, but are actually mammals.
They have lungs and breathe oxygen.

Bottlenose Dolphin

Dolphins speed through the sea, chasing fish. Sometimes
they like to leap out of the water, twisting and turning
their bodies as they fly through the air.

Kingfisher

You'll see a lightning-fast blur of blue and orange when a kingfisher dives into a river. This female plucks a fish from the water, then takes it to a nearby tree to eat.

Kingfisher parents need to catch more than 100 fish every day to feed their chicks.

Pink Salmon

The chilly river is churned up by hundreds of pink salmon thrashing around. They move up the busy river to calm water, where they will lay their eggs.

The salmon are almost crushed as they battle their way upriver.

Horses live in family groups called herds. They cross rivers to reach fields of grass and flowers.

Camargue Horse

These beautiful white horses gallop through many rivers in France. They enjoy the cool spray that splashes around them. Though they stay mostly on land, these wild horses are good swimmers.

Lesser Flamingo

Flamingos are dainty birds that love the water. They wade through lakes, scooping out food with their long, curved beaks. They have pink feathers because they eat pink food!

When a flamingo takes off, it runs along the water and spreads its long wings.

Caimans are reptiles, which means they have scaly skin. These caimans can grow to 2.8 metres long.

Yacare Caiman

When a caiman is hungry, it creeps silently into the water and waits for something tasty to swim by. Caimans have huge jaws and sharp teeth — perfect for snapping up piranha fish!

11

A wandering albatross measures up to 3.4 metres from wingtip to wingtip.

Wandering Albatross

This enormous bird is a wandering albatross. It glides above the oceans, dipping into the water to grab squid and fish to eat. His splashing scares smaller birds away!

This Indian tiger is at home in marshland. The land is boggy, but there are lots of places to swim.

Indian Tiger

Most cats hate water, but tigers love to splash, play and swim. Indian tigers chase deer — and even crocodiles — through marshes and rivers.

These apes love
to play with water.
They can scoop it
in their hands
to drink.

Orangutan

Young orangutans are smart animals that love to
explore their rainforest home. They spend most of their
lives in trees, eating juicy fruit. An orangutan's
toes can grip objects just like our fingers can.

Nile Crocodile

When a crocodile has its eyes on food,
it races through the water, splashing and crashing
its way to its prey. Those jaws can
snap shut in a second.

Crocodiles
belong to the
same family as
snakes, turtles
and dinosaurs.

Ospreys plunge feet first into water, grabbing fish with their talons.

Osprey

Ospreys are birds of prey. They have hooked beaks and sharp claws, called talons, for gripping slippery fish. Ospreys are also called fish hawks.

Capybara

Capybaras look like big guinea pigs. When the sun is hot they wallow in water to keep cool. Baby capybaras can swim just a few hours after they are born.

A capybara grows up to 1.2 metres long — that's bigger than many dogs!

Eurasian Coot

Coots have wide, webbed feet for walking through slushy mud. They have bad tempers and have been known to chase other birds away by splashing and kicking water at them!

When a coot wants to fly, it runs and flaps its wings.

Zebras often go on long journeys to find water to drink and sweet green grass to eat.

Plains Zebra

Zebras live in the hot African grasslands, where the sun shines all day. They must stay near a water hole or a river so they can drink.

Everyone likes playing in the bath! Young monkeys like to splash and swim.

Japanese Macaque

This macaque lives in a place where there are warm-water springs. He can choose a hot bath in the winter, or a cold river dip in the summer.

Olive Ridley Turtle

A female turtle clambers onto the shore to lay her eggs. The frothy waves help push her body onto the damp sand, where she will dig a burrow for her nest.

This is an olive ridley turtle. Like all sea turtles, she is an endangered animal.

Grey Wolf

This wolf's furry coat will keep him warm in winter, but not when it is soaking wet! When he stops running, he will shake, like a dog, to get himself dry.

This grey wolf uses his long, strong legs to leap through water.

Waves batter and splash this iguana, but he uses his toes to grip his rock.

Marine Iguana

Most lizards need to stay dry and bask in the hot sun, but marine iguanas are different. They like to get wet! They live by the sea and dive underwater to find food.

Red Lechwe

Red lechwe live in the African wetlands. They are water-loving antelopes that love to charge through water, splashing everything in sight!

Only male red lechwe antelopes have horns. They run when they are scared!

These quirky animals are related to kangaroos and koalas. They live by rivers and eat plants.

Quokka

Quokkas are very rare animals that live in Australia. They keep their babies in a pouch, like kangaroos and koalas. A quokka is about the same size as a cat.

Blue Wildebeest

Thousands of wildebeest gather in huge herds. Together they go on a long journey to find food. That journey takes the wildebeest across many fast-flowing rivers.

Wildebeest race across this shallow river because hungry crocodiles are lurking nearby.

Common Starling

Sprightly starlings can hop, skip and jump. They are busy, smart birds with shiny feathers. A quick dip in a puddle is a good way to keep those feathers looking lovely.

When a bird takes a bath, it keeps a beady eye open for cats!

Galapagos Sea Lion

During the daytime, sea lions are graceful dancers under the sea. At night, they haul their heavy bodies onto the shore to sleep.

Sea lions swim, swirl and splash in the cool ocean water.

A greylag goose ruffles his feathers, kicks his webbed feet and enjoys a shower!

Greylag Goose

Geese build their nests along riverbanks so they can slip into the water when they are hungry, or just want to swim. A baby goose is called a gosling.

Basilisks are such smooth movers, they only make tiny splashes.

Green Basilisk

A fast-moving basilisk scoots across the still pond water. He uses his tail to stay balanced. His broad feet help to spread his weight so he does not sink.

Orca

Orcas are a type of dolphin. An orca breathes through a hole on the top of her head. When orcas breathe out, they make a frothy spout of water.

An orca baby is called a calf. This calf is swimming alongside her mother.

Raindrops splash and splatter, but frogs don't mind the rain — they like getting wet.

Red-Eyed Tree Frog

A little red-eyed tree frog takes shelter from the rain.
These frogs live in forests where it rains most days,
so they are used to heavy downpours.

This lioness doesn't like having wet fur, so she shakes the water off.

African Lion

A lion is a deadly beast that usually hunts on land. Sometimes a lioness will jump into water, especially when she is chasing food for her cubs.

A hippo can be violent. Males use their huge jaws and big teeth to fight each other.

Hippopotamus

Hippos live in Africa and they spend most of the day wallowing at waterholes and in rivers. They need to keep their skin wet and muddy to stop it burning or cracking.

Grey Heron

A heron uses his super-sharp eyesight to see a wriggling fish underwater. He uses his long beak to quickly grab his slippery prey.

The fish is trapped, but it wriggles, flaps and splashes as it tries to escape!

There will be a massive splash when this whale hits the water! Large waves will move in all directions.

Humpback Whale

It takes great strength for a whale to leap out of the water. Humpback whales weigh as much as six elephants, but they are graceful animals.

Great Crested Grebe

These great crested grebes need to build a nest and lay some eggs. Before they build a home, these birds do a splash-dance and give each other gifts: a mouthful of pondweed!

Grebes swap gifts, sing and dance to show potential mates what good parents they will be.

Clawless Otter

A clawless otter has popped her head out of water, grabbing hold of a tasty treat. After a quick crunch the otter will disappear underwater again, searching for more crabs and fish to eat.

Clawless otters live in African lakes. Super-thick fur keeps the water off their skin.

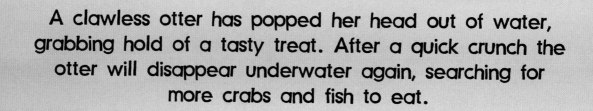

A grizzly is a type of large brown bear that lives in North America.

Grizzly Bear

A grizzly bear spins her head and water sprays in all directions.
Grizzlies are good swimmers and sit in shallow water, waiting
for their favourite food — salmon — to swim by.

Flying Fish

Most fish spend all their lives in water, but flying fish are more adventurous. They use their large, wing-like fins to skip across the water.

Flying fish make pretty splash patterns as they bounce over the ocean.

Common Goldeneye

This duck is putting on a special water dance. He bobs his head and splashes to make sure that all the other ducks notice how handsome he is.

Male goldeneyes have glossy, green heads, but females are not so colourful.

A walrus's tusks are teeth that can grow to 91 centimetres long.

Walrus

A male walrus grows so big he can barely move on land. In the water, he can roll, float, dip and dive like a synchronized swimmer. Walruses live in cool Arctic waters and they have flippers instead of legs.

Common Frog

When a frog is on land, he hops and crawls. In water, a frog becomes an amazing swimmer, stretching his body and using his long legs to glide silently beneath the surface.

This is a common green frog. He began his watery life as a little brown tadpole.

Great White Shark

Great white sharks patrol the oceans, looking for fish and seals to hunt. This shark is leaping out of the water to have a good look around before sinking beneath the waves.

The large dorsal fin on a shark's back helps him to swim quickly in a straight line.

These petrels are fighting over scraps of food. They eat any dead animals they find.

Petrels

These sea birds live in the Southern Ocean, near Antarctica. Northern giant petrels are huge, powerful birds that soar over the waves, looking for food.

Caribou

Life is hard for caribou. These deer live in icy lands near the Arctic. They go on long journeys, crossing rivers to find plants to eat. They are good swimmers.

Caribou are also known as reindeer.
Every year, males grow new antlers to be
used for fighting each other.

Seals have flippers, not legs. They spend their lives in the sea or resting on rocky shores.

Antarctic Fur Seal

This seal is rolling in the surf, enjoying the crash and tumble of waves. Its plump body is covered with a thick layer of fat, called blubber, and fur to keep it warm.

Come on everyone,
make a **SPLASH**!
The water's lovely!

Copyright © QED Publishing 2015

First published in the UK in 2015 by
QED Publishing
Part of The Quarto Group
The Old Brewery,
6 Blundell Street,
London,
N7 9BH

www.qed-publishing.co.uk

A catalogue record for this book is available from the British Library.

ISBN 978 1 78493 330 2

Printed in China

Picture Credits
(t=top, b=bottom, l=left, r=right, fc=front cover, bc=back cover)

Corbis bc and 48 Paul Souders, 34 © Anup Shah/Nature Picture Library
FLPA 6 Thomas Mangelsen/Minden Pictures, 8 Michael Quinton/Minden Pictures, 10 Elliott Neep, 11, 23, 28 Tui De Roy/Minden Pictures, 13 Mark Newman, 14 Konrad Wothe, 15 Frans Lanting, 17 Luciano Candisano/Minden Pictures, 18 IMAGEBROKER MICHAEL KRABS, Imag, 19 Frans Lanting, 20 Stephen Belcher/Minden Pictures, 21 Ingo Arndt/Minden Pictures, 22 Tim Fitzharris/Minden Pictures, 24 Frans Lanting, 25 Kevin Schafer/Minden Pictures, 26 Winfried Wisniewski/Minden Pictures, 27 Mathias Scchaef, BIA/Minden Pictures, 29 Malcom Schuyl, 31 Flip Nicklin/Minden Pictures, 32 Michael Durham/Minden Pictures, 40 Pierre Lobel/Biosphoto, 44 Gerard Lacz, 46 Winfried Wisniewski, 47 Hiroya Minakuchi/Minden Pictures
Getty fc toni, 2 Nick Garbutt/Minden Pictures, 4 Henrick Sorensen, 7 Mark Hughes, 9 Gallo Images:Danita Delimont, 12 Lonely Planet Images:David Tipling, 16 Oxford Scientific:Sven Zacek, 33 Floridapfe from S.Korea in cherl, 36 Sylvain Cordier, 37 David Tipling, 38 Mark Deeble and Victoria Store, 39 David G Hemmings, 41 Glenn Bartley, 42 Danita Delimont, 45 Oxford Scientific:David Tipling
National Geographic Creative 5 Paul Nicklen
Nature PL 30, 35 Bence Mate
Photoshot 3 Larry Ditto/NHPA, 43 Robert Pickett/NHPA